# Various Shades of Poetry

## by Corey Dixon

# Intro

P – Is for people and personal, in the different characters in bringing across my different views;

O – Outstanding, for breaking through a new field of moves;

E – Is to educate and elevate the mind of others, to bring a fun, exciting thrill;

T – Is for teaching and being tactful in the approach to display an array of skills;

R – Is for rectifying, reaching out, and revolutionizing others in a wonderful thing that's surely an art;

Y – Is the young to be influenced in this direction to make a new start;

This is an introduction to what you will read.

# Chapter 1

**Corey Dixon**

# Mask or Masquerade

People wear masks to run away from incident, accident, and even their self,

Like they are the only one who's flawed and should be put on the shelf.

Some people wear masks to guard themselves from the public nation;

They are the ones who will do anything to preserve their self-reputation.

You also have a few who throw a false projection

To keep you from learning what's their mask, to ration themselves out in sections.

A lot of people wear masks out of protection and fear;

Can you tell the real reason you brought our mask and showed you hear?

The people that deal with mask wearers often get pushed in a different direction;

Every time they are in an area of the subjection.

# Various Shades of Poetry

Once the mask is off you can deal with the real issues,

On working through the problem to get to the other side of the venue.


Some people wear masks so long it becomes attached to their face;

The real them may be lost forever, no sign of a trace.


No healing can get through because the mask blocks out the air;

To override the mask, you must want it for yourself and push it off of there.

# A Bitter Sweet Ending

Naomi starts out losing her husband and two little mans,

Oprah and Ruth were left with her as their journey began.

Naomi told her in-laws to go back from where they came,

Oprah followed her instruction while Ruth's decision remained unchanged.

While going to Bethlehem Naomi changed her name to Bitter (Mara),

Even in turmoil Naomi and Ruth didn't become quitters.

Naomi had a wealthy kinsman name Boaz,

Ruth was instructed to worked in the fields while servants told him she was from Moab.

Ruth asked Boaz to work and gleam,

Boaz agreed to let her joined the team.

Ruth came back to Naomi's to tell her the news,

Naomi instructed her on the next field of moves.

That same night Ruth went to Boaz to lie down and covered his feet,

Boaz told her remain tonight so she can go to sleep.


Next day Boaz went to the elders of the city

To discuss the family inheritance of Naomi and Ruth in their respected cities.


Boaz bought all the land and made Ruth his wife,

Over time they conceived a son that Naomi fed in her bosom, blessing her and the little tyke.


Naomi didn't let her personal feeling stop her to invest,

She did the right thing for Ruth that brought out the best.

Corey Dixon

# Birthdays

Birthdays are a celebration that comes around annually

Just to let you know you're getting older gradually.

Birthdays make you reflect on growing up,

You never can think about them enough.

Some people celebrate birthdays with various events,

While little kids have slumber parties and sleep inside or outside in tents,

Many people receive gifts, clothes, cake, and candles,

Other people receive weird gifts that should be put behind the mantle.

So when your time comes around, enjoy your special day

Always have fun because it's your birthday!

**Various Shades of Poetry**

# Mothers Around the World

Moms should be the real heroes of the world today,
While majority of guys leave them with a load of responsabil-a-tae,
Always want to run when they cannot have their way,
However, child support catches them in the sorry attempt of a getaway.
Some moms are working two jobs and are making things happen,
Other moms are playing both mom and dad roles so you can call them the captain.
All mothers should want to be like a friend,
Because we always need you to the very end.
Never underestimate a mother's strength when it comes down to their children's care,
That natural instinct smells sweeter than the honey that's in the air.
Knowing that no matter how bad you mess up they will always be there,
Even if you drove them crazy to a point of wanting to pull out their hair.
Mothers are more than a soldier and are extremely tough,
Even when at times you may feel that they were way too rough.

Moms are really looking out for your best interests,
So you won't have to learn the hard way the mistakes of your consequences.
This if for moms and soon-to-be moms around,
You are the ones that really deserve the crown.

**Corey Dixon**

# Giving It Your All

When you are giving something your all
Rest assured some type of evil will try to get you to fall,

They will at least try to slow you down to crawl
Or attack your emotions to get you angry and brawl,

Haters hate to see your passion and focus,
If negativity can take that away you will feel hopeless.

Giving it your all increases your chance of meeting success,
Giving it your all through your struggle always brings out the best.
When giving it your all to what you're doing,
You don't worry about what others think 'cause you're too busy pursuing.
If you're not giving your all you may encounter some unbalance,
You may find that it's harder to overcome a negative challenge.
Giving your all is something that you have to determine,
This is not a lecture, more like a poetical sermon.

# Reaping a Bad Harvest

Abimelech played with fire, and fire struck back,

He hired worthless men to do evil, to help him attack.

Abimelech went to Ophrah to slaughter his seventy brothers,

But Jotham, the youngest, left and hid from his older brother.

The men of Shechem then made Abimelech king,

Jotham spoke against him, saying that Shechem did the wrong thing.

Abimelech reigned for three years, which is a short amount of time,

God sent an evil spirit between him and Shechem to pay for his crime:

The men of Shechem went out to ambush the king in the mountain top.

Gad and Ebed were two people trying to put this reign to a stop,

The two men were talking about how the king got on their nerves.

Zebul, the city mayor, sent a message to the king of what he overheard,

Abimelech then set up a plan to overtake the crew.

He ambushed all of them that were there and smote the first two of Gad and Ebed,

Abimelech was told that the other people were headed to Shechem tower,

**Corey Dixon**

He wasn't going to stop until he took all of their power:

Abimelech's plan was to set the tower on fire.

He had a thousand people waiting for them, from knight to the squires,

The king arrived at the tower and drew near the door,

A woman dropped an upper milestone on his head as Abimelech fell to the floor.

The king asked his arm bearer to slay him so people wouldn't think the woman did,

Thus God repaid Abimelech for all his wickedness.

**Various Shades of Poetry**

# Noah's Ark

The Lord regretted He made man on earth because they were wicked,

All living creatures were about to be blotted out, and evicted.


God found favor in Noah and told him to build an ark,

Noah had to collect two of every animal, clean and unclean, and set them apart.


Noah warned the people and preached about their sinful abuse,

Yet they rejected God and were without an excuse.


The Lord said in seven days I will cause it to rain for forty days and forty nights,

Every living substance will be wiped away, no one left in sight.


Noah was six hundred years old when the floodgates of Heaven were opened,

Once the people saw the rain they realized that Noah wasn't jokin'.


When the Lord closed the ark, decision time was a little bit too late,

**Corey Dixon**

Now the wicked could do nothing but face their fate.

Water was so high that the high hills were covered,

Everything on land was completely smothered.

It actually took a year and ten days to dry the entire land,

Noah built the ark to carry out God's plan.

# Anniversary

What does the word 'anniversary' mean to you?
As a matter of fact, I'll give you a clue:

Anniversaries are filled with memories that make you look back,
To see how well you kept things together and intact.

Anniversaries consist of yearly achievements, friendship, or togetherness,
Anniversaries are something you don't want to ever miss.

Anniversaries are full of celebrations,
It's good to see progress on your own working creation.

Anniversaries come often, but they are certainly not easy,
It takes constant work in what you're doing to see fulfillment, please believe me.

A lot of people have never experienced one,
They either jump ship or haven't found their special one.

So on your anniversary, go out, have a ball,
It's a celebration, remember, so give it your all!

**Corey Dixon**

# 90's

Remember when sex themes were introduced to businesses?

Now you can't see an ad without someone showing off their nakedness.

What about news back then, like Rodney King and OJ running away in the Bronco truck?

On a peaceful side, events like the Million Man March, where no one was shot or struck.

How about TV sitcoms like *Fresh Prince*, *Martin*, *Steve Harvey*, *Living Single*, and many more?

Up until that time that was some of the best shows we've seen before.

What about industry-changing movies like *Boyz n the Hood*, *New Jack City*, *Juice*, *Coming to America* and *Waiting to Exhale*?

That era produced opportunity for many upcoming actors, as far as I can tell.

Remember when the East Coast vs. West Coast rivalry was really big?

The rap industry lost two of the best rappers, Biggie and 2Pac, in that mess you dig.

> What about when Bad Boys, No Limit, and Cash Money had the industry locked with their run at a dynasty, Death Row and N.W.A held it down in the early 80's/90's,

Remember when Jay-Z took over hip hop and carried the torch?

Which mic review could be seen in a magazine called *The Source*?

**Various Shades of Poetry**

What about clothes like Cross Colours, Nautical, Tommy, and daisy dukes were in,

How about the bright-colored hair, braids, and yarn braids that started to grow trends?

Remember when Sony Playstation came to gaming and first hit the scene,

While the Nintendo 64 was left in the shadows, going unseen?

Even in sports, remember when the Bulls went on three peats,

Or when the USA team in the Olympics never carried a defeat?

Man, the 90's sure had some opportunities that were sweet,

If you missed them, you must been busy, a coma, or just asleep.

Corey Dixon

# Plantation Farm

The place I work

Feels like I'm on the plantation field picking cotton, shoveling dirt.

Every day you learn about a new restriction,

While other employees are getting fired like a past due eviction;

Being watched more than an inmate with ten convictions,

Some people fold from stress 'cause it's hot in this kitchen;

Where people always looking to steadily advance,

While the fake people are itching to get in your pants.

Corp American slogan goes like this: You scratch my back, I stab you in yours,

I'm trying to make money off you and do as little as possible with the task or chores.

You also see managers here with the hospitality of a Southern granny,

But the real status is the identity of Uncle Tom or Sammy.

**Various Shades of Poetry**

Everyone can see their foundation is shaky,

Trying to outsource jobs for cheap to little Akbar and Su Hi Cheng that loves to play with little sticky pasties.

Who knows working about working a 9-to-5?

Trying to battle with a bully called Life and just trying to survive,

Every couple of months you have a corporate meeting,

While listening to corporate executives sounding retarded when they are stupidly speaking;

They can't even answer one question about one simple thing,

But can tell you how to do your job like it's nothing.

Now I hope by writing I didn't do anyone harm,

Oops, it is my time to leave the plantation farm.

**Corey Dixon**

# Samson

The angel of the Lord told Manoah and his wife that they would bear a son,

The power that he'll possess will become second to none.

Samson saw one of the daughters of Philistine,

He asked his parents to retrieve her because she thought she was fine.

In Timnah a young lion rose against Samson,

He tore the lion so fast you would have thought it was a phantom.

Samson went to talk with the woman and it pleased him well,

He told the thirty companions a riddle that he unveiled,

Samson gave them seven days to get the reply,

The men of the city told Samson's wife to entice him, to get the answer without a try.

Once she got the answer, she told her country men,

Samson slew thirty men in Ashkelon with his bare hands.

**Various Shades of Poetry**

On the eighth day Samson's wife was given to his friend,
Samson repaid the Philistines with revenge:

Samson caught three hundred foxes and torched their tails,
He let run through the Philistine grain as they caught fire and fell.

The Philistines found Samson was behind the act,
So they pursued him until they go their payback.

Samson went to Judah and the Philistines followed, too,
Judah decided to come against Samson, to help out the Philistine crew.

Judah took Samson to Lehi as he agreed to be bound,
He broke free once he heard the people of Philistine.

The spirit of the Lord came down on him mightily,
Once he was free, he slew a hundred men with a bone of a donkey.

Samson went to Gaza, saw a harlot, and went into her,
A lot of men can learn a lesson from this biblical adventure.
After this he loved a woman from the valley of Sorek
Who was offered 1,100 pieces of silver to subdue him with her

# Corey Dixon

intellect.

Delilah asked Samson where his strength lies, So we can subdue you.

Why would anyone mess with a woman out to get you?

She was so persistent over time

Samson told her eventually and became blind.

They shaved his head, Samson became weak,

Bored out his eyes so he couldn't take a peak.

Over time Samson's hair grew back,

The Philistines thought their god Dagon was all that.

They brought Samson out of prison for sport,

God never leaves His people inside a fort.

The stadium was filled with three thousand or so,

Samson prayed between the pillars to have vengeance on his foes.

Samson pushed the pillars with the regained strength,

The whole stadium fell out, no one was left in that tent.

Samson did this task without doubt or fear,

Samson judged Israel for approximately twenty years.

# Giving Up

The road may be rough,

The journey may be tough,

Never think for a second about giving up.

If you quit now that means it's the end of the show,

Leaving uncertainty on how much farther you had to go.

Quitters really don't prosper,

They never reach achievements, like obtaining an Oscar.

The area you quit will have a question mark,

Your ultimate goal will fade away in the dark.

All you can do is talk about what you could've done,

Sounding like you chose to lose when you could have won.

You see what happens when someone gives up,

All you can do is hang in there and try not to be stuck in the same rut.

**Corey Dixon**

# Cars, Pt 1

Some people are very proud of being a vehicle owner,

Even treat their cars like their kids, never a donor.

Some people dress their car up like a kid that puts on clothes,

Always excited when they get something new, as if it never gets old.

Some people are collectors of old cars and antiques,

While others rely on newer versions that are faster and more sleek.

They don't make models like they used to,

Nowadays you always have to replace a part or two.

Other people give cars baths one to four times a week,

Then go and protect their car from outside by wrapping them up in sheets.

If it weren't for car transportation, we would definitely be crippling,

Cars make going a lot easier, I wish more things were this simple.

# God is Good

God is good all the time, and all the time God is good.

Why don't some people seem to understand?

Is it because some don't understand He is the divine power of the Master that created the universe and man?

God is good because He looks out for every man in every neighborhood

'God is good' can be defined as a characteristic of God,

How is He good to you? I can answer that with no problem, Todd.

God is good when you're broke but have a roof on your head and clothes on your back,

That's a blessing by itself, by itself, and can be taken as a fact.

Even if you don't have the necessities, you're alive and able to breathe,

With that alone I know my lungs feel relieved.

God is good because He is God,

He can defeat anything, especially the status quo odds.

**Corey Dixon**

God also has a father characteristic and wants to take care of you,

Even if you're going through tough times and can't see His views.

If I had to write all the reasons why God is good, my time would definitely pass away.

Just realize that God is good, not once, but in all ways.

# Summer

This time of year people encounter a lot of sun,

Most high school and college students would agree summer is the best time to have fun.

Some people throw get togethers, family reunions, and take a couple trips,

Others try to cool off in the pool by taking a few dips.

Teachers and students have three months to get away,

Many people have to work, while others go off and play.

You can also do numerous physical sport activities,

Like B-ball, football, working out, track, and tennis courts at parks that are over the vicinity.

Summer is filled with a lot of long days and very long nights,

Especially if you have an outing looking into the night.

You also have a lot of celebrity events and various car shows,

You always have fun when you go to one of those.

**Corey Dixon**

Summer is always a great time to cool off and relax,

That's why I decided to grab a pen and put this on wax (paper).

Various Shades of Poetry

# Independence Day

This is a holiday that's celebrated throughout the United States
To reflect on Independence Day, July 4th, 1776, was the actual date.

Most family and friends get together for all types of parties and parades,
The food will be barbeque with a liquid beverage, Kool-Aid.

On this day most businesses acknowledge the holiday,
Getting paid for work and being off is special any day.

You can't forget about all the different state and local fairs,
Whether you're down there for rides, funnel cakes, or just to take the little ones in their stroller chairs.

It's normally hot, you may see some cut tops and halter-top shirts,
But a lot of people enjoy seeing the display of fireworks.

Whether you see the fireworks at the parade or popping your own right down the block,
A lot of people enjoy Independence Day, believe it or not.

**Corey Dixon**

# Daily Devotion

Dear Father, there is none like that can come close to you in the whole universe,

You're all I need to succeed and be excellent in you.

> You're everything—problem solving, blessing, wisdom, and much more—the names are endless, times infinity.

You are the best as I trust and rely in you for all wants and needs,

As well I must continue to give my all to be made whole in you.

You are my Dad as well as best friend,

I continually put praises in my mouth of you about you.

So no more worrying about issues because you can handle all issues,

So as the doors may continually to be opened up for me through you,

I rely on you to achieve your purpose in me for a win-win.

**Various Shades of Poetry**

# Pooky Alert

As we're doing our daily work,

We have to notify each other when it's time for a pooky alert.

You must prepare for pooky and their kin,

Making sure you apply on some thick skin.

If you don't apply it can trigger an emotion to make you lose your job,

So we notify each other so no one is asked to leave with a sob.

Pooky has a characteristic like loud, broken English and a lot of anger,

Always in a rush, like the inmate is going somewhere, or in danger.

I know some of these pooky folk had to go to school,

But you can tell English wasn't their strongest tool.

Why do they send money to a company that they set up, any accounts or nothing, and want to know who dropped the ball?

Sometimes you argue back and forward, like "Operator's Revenge."

**Corey Dixon**

    That depends on if they are talking stupid and if their voice ascends,

That's why we have people here, strong and sharper than a laser beam.

We now formed a resistance group proudly called the Pooky Alert Team.

# Babies

A new baby is definitely a blessing,

Some woman will do anything from fertilizing eggs to other methods, for this is an obsession.

Babies make you learn and relearn a few lessons,

Some become overwhelmed, they start stressing.

Babies that come to the earth need all the help in the world,

Whether it's Momma's little boy or Daddy's little girl.

Some babies make you laugh, others make you sigh,

Babies will produce that good feeling that can't be duplicated, only multiplied.

Babies are like a chia pet as you watch them grow,

Some people say they grow up too fast, other days it's too slow.

All babies are no accident and come with purpose and reason,

Even if you feel you are not ready, you have nine months to prepare for the baby's season.

**Corey Dixon**

# The Band

When you go to a football game, I can tell you the best place in the land,

It's not really a seat or section, it's playing in the band.

The band combines of woodwinds, brass, and the popular percussion,

Though some feel quite nervous and scared, their head spinning as if they had a concussion.

In the band you have position, chairs, and all in rank,

When you first start, you have had a funny name, or even been the butt of a prank.

Band is hard work when you're up at 6am for practice formation,

But it's all worth it when you see the crowd's participation.

Once you put that uniform on you know you are all united,

That's when the players get excited.

## Various Shades of Poetry

At this point some people may or may not really understand,

All—members, ex-members, and current members—have pride in their marching band.

Corey Dixon

# Father's Day

Fathers are the leader and the head of household,

Fathers are supposed to teach their kids valuable lessons they can use when they get old.

When a father walks in his child's room, he's acknowledged with much respect,

You rarely see a kid do the opposite, like rebel or reject.

When some kids see their dad, it immediately reminds them of authority and power,

Some kids view their dad as a superhero that's skiing over towers.

Father's role in a child's relationship is something that can't be replaced,

The dad, most times, is the disciplinarian that has to get in their face.

A father and son combo is hard to ignore,

You are seen as your dad, and your mini-me is standing next to you on the floor.

**Various Shades of Poetry**

So cherish those father moments each and every day,

Once you get grandpa status, you have something to look to once you become old and gray.

Corey Dixon

# The Story and Thoughts of Adam and Eve

In the Garden of Eden resided Adam and Eve,
Who wound up being fooled and deceived.

God told Adam, You can have anything you see, but
Don't eat any fruit from the Knowledge of Good and Evil Tree.

Before the Fall, Adam and Eve were perfectly in tune with God,
The devil fused a plan together to get Adam and Eve dislodged.

I think the devil knew he couldn't approach Adam or his plan would sink,
Instead he infiltrated Adam by tricking Eve, who was the weakest link.

Adam had power and rank, and named every creature, including Eve,
That's what I'm sticking with and truly believe.

With Adam and Jesus, the devil used someone close to them to do his dirty deed,

**Various Shades of Poetry**

To inject a demonic plan in the weak, to project a bad seed.

After Eve was tricked she ate of the fruit; Adam proceeded to follow,

It was Adam's job to keep responsibility and protect, how could he be so shallow?

This is a brief discussion of the fall of man,

Jesus in the end will win according to plan.

**Corey Dixon**

# Lies

I really don't understand why
Some people have a habit to lie.
When some people lie, it's really pointless,
Making them feel dislodged, as if they are jointless.
Some lie just 'cause they don't have nothing better to do,
They tell on themselves, in the process by giving you a clue.
Lies are nothing but an amplified goose chase
That are often smooth but slick and told at a fast pace.

When lies are exposed they make matters worse,
Lies may sometime carry only a spiritual curse.

Lies are truth's biggest contender,
White lies can't cover a small dent in a car fender.

If you tell one lie, you may have to tell more,
Every time you talk about a topic, you will dish out lies as if they were stock at a store.

**Various Shades of Poetry**

Lies at first may feel like they have a purpose,

But in the end they lead to a brick wall that makes lies worthless.

Lies are statements that definitely can't stand,

If you have to answer for them, you really don't stand a chance.

Corey Dixon

# Spring

You know when you are approaching spring,
It's the time you wake up to birds that sing.

Spring is where it's not too cold or hot,
It's the perfect weather that will definitely hit the spot.

Spring is where you do see a lot more days and a lot less night,
But you can do more activities that revolve around the light.

Spring is also a time for homeowners to do their spring cleaning
So their houses can be filled with a dose of gleaming.

Spring does have a negative side that makes you lose an hour of sleep,
You have a lot of nicer days to let your top down or cruise in your Jeep.

You have to watch spring when it comes to April showers,
However, rain is always good for the flowers.
Springtime is preparing for the summer heat,
Most people think that's the best time, that can't be beat.

**Various Shades of Poetry**

# 80's

This current time the world is certainly crazy,

So let me give you my presentation of the 80's:

Remember big pop stars like Madonna and Cindy Lauper that wore the color blonde?

I remember when the in famous shoe was Pro Wings, Adidas, and Cons.

What about favorite girls' names—Keisha, Iesha, a few named Myrtle?

Naw, I remember not missing an episode of the *Teenage Mutant Ninja Turtles.*

Look how things change from now to then, it certainly got harder,

I remember when people died for wearing Jordans and the coats that were made by Starter.

Check out how you can now play life-like video games and even drive Benzos,

I agree, nothing compares with *Super Mario Brothers* on the 8-bit Nintendo.

Remember people like LL Cool J and Big Daddy Kane?

Now people brag about being shot up like it's good—isn't that insane?

Don't you remember watching TV shows like *Amen, 227,* and *The Cosby Show?*

Yeah, they don't play things like that anymore, that has morals and goals.

Remember the people who wore them big gold chains,

**Corey Dixon**

That also had the hi-top box and thought they were doing the thang?

When we were kids we just had a ball,

Now being grown some situations just make you want to run up a wall.

For you 80's people, just wanted to take you back to the nostalgia days,

We're all just older kids with more responsibility anyways.

## Ms. Inform

Late one night I saw a car commercial,

It was done so proficient that they had to practice in a few rehearsals.

The dealer says 99 bucks down today

And you will be guaranteed to drive off the lot right away,

The dealer says all credit good and bad are already approved,

I knew it was shaky, but boy did it sound smooth,

Dealer says just bring a valid license and two check stubs to show work history proof,

By this time I was high fivin' the ceiling and raising the roof.

After commercial I knew this place would see me tomorrow,

My issues would be solved, not an ounce of me was filled with sorrow.

**Corey Dixon**

Midday came and I was finally here,

I walked on the lot with a McDonald's smile that was bright and clear.

The dealer says, "Pick what you want, then come see me,"

I say, "Sure thing," as I sounded so happily.

I picked out the car and went to the man,

That's when my plan sifted in my hands, just like I was holding sand.

Dealer says we need to go in and fill out some paperwork,

I thought, If they do a credit report, they will see all my dirt.

I looked through the paperwork that was in the dealer's hand,

My arch-nemesis, Mr. Credit Report, showed up; I said, "Ain't that grand."

Luckily for me, I knew what I saw and heard on the commercial,

I filled out the forms and hoped it wasn't going to be controversial.

The dealer took the paperwork and said, "I'll be back,"

# Various Shades of Poetry

I wanted to say, "Have my keys ready," as a matter of fact.

Five minutes later he came and said,

"Sir, you only qualify for a Geo Metro;" I replied, "The one that sounds like a moped?"

I said, "This commercial was too good to be true. I've should've known this plan wasn't going to flow;"

The dealer said, "My man, did you see the small print on the bottom?" I responded like Homer Simpson: D'oh.

The dealer said, "I didn't mean to sound a storm,

But you need to pay attention a little better because you was 'Miss Informed.'"

So as I go home you'll probably wonder why it sounds like I left with a crowd,

I left in the Metro that sounded loud.

Corey Dixon

# Truth

The truth hurts because it's known to set people free,

The truth is also some people's enemy.

The truth is all good because it comes from inside,

Some get nervous around him as if they'll jump off this ride.

Truth brings you to a point to where you no longer can hide,

The truth brings some folk back from reality as some may have felt hurt and cried.

Truth doesn't get along with pride,

If you get along with truth you will begin to make strides.

When truth meets lies they often collide,

Some can't handle truth pressures as they make an attempt at suicide.

Jesus is the way, truth and the light,

I thought I would try to bring home a different sight.

## Various Shades of Poetry

Truth can be hard, but it's the only way to go,

This here is the truth, ladies and gents, so I figure I will let you know.

# **Bible**

B – Is for brilliant biography of letters that were wrote;

I – Is for illustrious, infallible, intelligence people who lack knowledge, this would be their antidote;

B – Benevolent blueprint for believing in various covenant promises and to have ammunition of words;

L – Is for servants to be levelheaded, longstanding for lie's bad situations that you have encountered, this book is used to lift you up, to stay superb;

E – Edification, the essential for an eternal salvation that we are all trying to get.


That's why this book is the bestselling book in the universe and always will remain to be a number-one hit.

# Champions

Champions are people who made it from struggling,

Even when their blood pressure was bubbling.

Champions most times never have an easy way out,

Always focus on goals, no room for doubt.

Champions have a characteristic that isn't inherited,

They always maintain their word and keep their merits.

Some champions are thankful and humble just to advance to part two,

They don't forget about where they came from or what they've been through.

In a crowd champions stand out like a different texture,

Most can handle the heat and be cool under pressure.

Champions are the best people to learn from,

Always positive while adding to your own sum.

**Corey Dixon**

Champions know it's hard to stay on top,

That's why they keep working 'cause they are the ones people look up to and watch.

# Operator's Revenge

"Hi, this Tony from Whacky Communications,
We currently serve a million-plus customers around the nation,

"Go ahead please." "Well, um, umm, I don't know who you really be,
But why my phone don't accept collect calls for Rashad Pooky."

"Well, ma'am, I know you're mad, but can you please calm down,"
But in my head I knew she was about to clown.

As I put her on mute, I ask, "Does she know how stupid she sounds?"
I continued to listen while shaking my head in dismay with a frown.

So as she finish yapping away,
I say, "Ma'am, can you shut up? I have something to say."

She responds with "Who you talking to?" I say, "The person on the other end."
I knew to ring the bell and let the fight began.

**Corey Dixon**

I say with a fierce voice, "Have you called the prison customer service?"

She says, "Oh, do you have their number?" but responds shy and nervous.

I say, "Ma'am, you should listen first before you blow up and react."

I felt like P. Diddy Combs saying "Take that, take that, take that!"

Now, the customer pushed me to the lines of disrespect,

I can't help that her brain was on the age of nine with the sounds of a dumb intellect.

So often after a couple rounds of back and forward, I had to set her straight,

Call me Tony the Tiger 'cause I sure felt GRRREAT!

When it was all over, the customer apologized and wanted to make amends,

Look out for the sequel, "Pooky Alert," on the next operator's revenge.

# Construction Skit

A car drove down a dark road and saw a construction sign,

But the lady didn't see anyone and just figure it was fine.

She continued to drive until she seen a block in the path,

But only seen one worker and figure something's up 'cause she did her math.

So she asked, "Is there constriction here?" He said, "Yeah, it just begun."

She's thinking, How is this possible when she only sees a person of one?

The woman continued to probe and said, "Well, what are you about to do?"

He said, "I'm plugging up holes in the street and won't be done until they're all through."

The woman had seen all these construction lights around,

Took a closer look while continuing to look down.

She said, "With all due respect, sir, there is nothing wrong with

**Corey Dixon**

the road as far as I can see."

He said, "I know, sweetheart, this problem you can't see visually."

The woman was standing there looking perplexed and confused
While the man had a smile on his face as if he was amused.

As she shook her head, she had nothing to say,
He told her, "Before you go to bed, make sure you pray."

The lady agreed to the man with a silent "Okay,"
She saw him in the rearview mirror as she drove away.

The next morning came, she woke up from her sleep
But was greeted with the sound of an alarm clock that went *beep*!

As she rushed to her car, she drove away,
Not realizing she took the same road she took yesterday.

What a relief, she thought, to see the road was free,
She continued to drive down the road fast but yet swiftly.

**Various Shades of Poetry**

She looked on the side of the car, and her eyes met up with an eighteen-wheeler truck,

The driver lost control, all she could do was duck.

Seconds later she was able to see,

Not a mark was done or damage to her entire body.

Later on that day, she saw the accident on TV

As the person from last night appeared and spoke to her gently.

She said, "I knew something about that conversation seem to be odd."

He said, "Earlier today you receive a blessing, a miracle from God."

"Since you did just as you were told,

God will bless you from this day until you are well and old."

She said, "Thank you, God, for all you have done,

No matter how hard the devil tries to defeat me, in you I already won."

**Corey Dixon**

# Chapter 2

# Judas

These are the characteristics of a man name Judas

Who betrayed Christ: Others, but definitely was foolish

To become an informer for the enemy and set up a conclave,

Then had to pay the eternal price once he was put in his grave.

To have the audacity to betray, disrespect Him with a kiss on the

Cheek,

The enemy better be glad Jesus was on a mission and wasn't going to stop

Until it was complete.

Just to think to turn on the son of God for a measly thirty shekels of

Silver,

You know that had to be demonic influence in order to get Judas

Bewilder.

This shows that people will do anything for an earthly advance,

Even sell their soul for cheap just to fall in the trap like quick

Sand.

Once the damage was done, he went and tried to hide

With a mentality so unstable he went to commit suicide.

**Various Shades of Poetry**

Now this is the epitome example of being disloyal,

That's why he is being tortured on foreign soil.

He now lives with a decision that he will always regret,

People perish because some don't operate out of their spiritual intellect.

# The Basis of Completeness

This poem is just a format of what you can use in your own situation. The format is as follows: Get scriptures that you need help or strength in, and put them at the top of your prayer. Next, give a reason of what each verse means to you. Then give your reason for why you are praying. After doing that, give some more supported Bible verses that will be beneficial to your situation, and then close it out. Here's an example:

Lord, I come to you today before the Throne under these following scriptures:

1. I give my burden to the Lord, and He will take care of me (Assurance);

2. I set my mind and keep it set on what is above the higher things, not the earth (Mind);

3. He becomes poor who works with slack and idle hand, but the hand of the diligent make riches (Diligence);

4. Walk in obedience (Discipline);

5. The Lord causes my enemy who rises up against me to be defeated before my face;

6. I Trust and rely in and was confident in you, O Lord, I say you are my God, my times are in your hands (Belief).

**Various Shades of Poetry**

Here is an example of a reason:

Lord, I call on you, you're my upper hand,

Please instruct and guide me in wisdom to let me understand;

As I ask that your purpose in me is my plan,

Please instruct and guide me in wisdom to let me understand;

As I ask that your purpose in me is my plan

To follow the straight and narrow road, I give all that I can;

Continue to keep me low as you remain high,

Jesus, you're the only person I can trust and rely;

Here you can support on your already foundation scriptures, like

If God is with me, who can be against me?

Your word has never failed or come back with a void on it,

I have victory wherever I go, then you finish out there.

In Jesus' name I pray these things to you, in your name, amen,

To follow the straight and narrow road I give all that I can.

Continue to keep me low as you remain high

Jesus, you're the only person I can trust and rely.

Here you can support on your already foundation scriptures:

**Corey Dixon**

If God is with me, who can be against me?

Your word has never failed or come back with a void on it,

I have victory wherever I go,

Then you finish out there.

In Jesus' name I pray these things to you, in your name.

# Stereotype

A man was on his way to a

store on a late Friday night

And was suddenly approached with a circulation of lights.

His natural thought was should he run or stay cool?

He figured Option A wouldn't work 'cause they would beat him like Kunta, and he wasn't going to be the fool.

The officer came to the car and asked him to step out for a minute,

As the officer called for backup, he was hoping this was Ashton Kutcher's show *Punk'd*,

But it didn't feel like it was a gimmick.

Officer Knight came and said, "There was a burglary in the area, and you fit the description."

He said, "You have the wrong one, I'm on my way to the store to pick up my wife's medical prescription."

He said, "I don't mean any disrespect to you, Officer Knight,

### Corey Dixon

But please don't judge me by my appearance, that is a stereotype."

When the officer walked away, he turned and struck him with all his might,

He got beat so bad he thought that he was going into the light.

He did feel bad, 'cause little did they know,

That the guy was an executive producer of a national TV show.

The next day he went to report the bad boys in blue,

You know he was going to receive a fat ole check 'cause he was going to sue.

The question I have is, I know the police look at our race like the apple doesn't fall too far from the tree,

But why do majority of good people get stung by that bumblebee?

I blame some of us, as I do them,

The ones that resemble this negative type that can be seen in your next big ghetto film.

As a whole you can never stay strong if your own is helping cut down the limbs,

**Various Shades of Poetry**

That's partially some of the reason the gutface was kissing the officer's Timbs.

Too many people focus on the wrong image rather than right,

Well, these are just my thoughts for this poem, so have a good night.

**Corey Dixon**

# Rules

Love them, hate them, we all have to follow them,

In most cases you have to acknowledge them.

These specific things might have a name called rules,

If you don't follow them, then you may wind up being the fool.

Everything in the universe has a particular structure

That ties in to our normal infrastructure.

Rules have been around before you came into understanding,

Once you become of age, some people act like they are so demanding.

Rules are throughout the entire nation,

They are even found in the way we conduct conversations.

Rules are nothing but an instruction and orders to obey,

So if you don't like them, get over it, OK?

# The Sheppard

The Sheppard looks out for all and protects his flock,

The Sheppard makes time for all so none will feel left out of his stock.

The Sheppard feeds, cleans, heals, and sometimes carries his sheep,

When he moves, they move; as one, as if they were a fleet.

When a sheep gets away too many times, the Sheppard breaks his leg because they were non-compliant,

This discipline actually is a solution for the sheep as they become reliant.

The Sheppard also chases away the sheep's prey,

Even if one was dragged off, he's off to bring him back that same day.

The sheep should be the Sheppard's best friend,

One who won't leave his sheep until the very end.

# Dream (Vision)

D – Is to distinguish your goals and task;

R – Rigorous, to keep pushing past reality's standards; as long as you believe in yourself, the standards won't last;

E – To be enthusiastic because you will need to bring your spirits up as they fall down;

A – Is to accept nothing less from anyone, especially if others are trying to hold you to the ground;

M – Is for Mammon to have wealth from accomplishing your dream while expanding yourself; don't repeat the circle, that's not working and causing you to drown.

Dreams are something a lot of people follow and try to obtain,

This is a motivational poem to keep you going even if you're struggle-lain!

## What's in You

Whatever is in you will certainly come out,

Is it God or evil in you, or do you have doubts?


Out of the abundance of the heart, the mouth will speak,

Do you know what way to go to get the answer you seek?


It's true that you are known by the fruit of your works,

This is one way you can tell if it's good or nothing but dirt.


Do you have a desire to do good, better, or a desire to do wrong?

Do you at least attempt to keep the commandments of God the Master that sits on the throne?


Do you pray and read, or just read and play,

Do you know the book that can help save you today?

Do you really love God or do you care about yourself,

Are you really interested in your spiritual health?

So by asking yourself these questions, you can do a personal diagnostic

To make sure you're not carrying any poisonous toxics.

**Corey Dixon**

Do you want to build a foundation or just play in soil,

Do you want to have an abundant life minus all the turmoil?

That's only one question now that comes to a perspective view,

Do you know what resides in you?

# The Predator

Some people are the predator, others are the prey;

We are going to discuss them all today.

Predators do nothing but look for prey

Because they don't want to improve themselves the regular hard way.

Predators plan a strategy before they loom

To see what prey they can hunt and consume.

A predator's candidate is someone who may be weak,

They use their game and talk meek (sweet).

Predator's strength is to use someone else as a stepping stone,

When they are alone predators are like newborns.

Predators are dumb and smart but definitely stay lurking,

They don't care about the victim that they are hurting.

Predators destroy bridges and even tell lies

By coming to you in need as if you're an ally.

Predators act like a host that's connected to a parasite,

The wound will only hurt if you continue to let the host bite.

If a predator would invest that planning and strategy in themselves

## Corey Dixon

They would see that they don't have to misuse anyone to achieve advancement and wealth.


Bonus: Do you think some predators fear their own goals and being rejected

And feel they have a better chance on preying on a friend by intercepting them?

## **Repercussion of Peer Pressure**

There was a boy named Lawrence, who always wanted to fit in,

He was looking for acceptance of having friends.

Lawrence was weak against peer pressure, so he was easily influenced,

This problem was riding his back like a nuisance.

Lawrence found some so-called friends that thought of him as a joke,

This was in the 80's, when the big drug of the time was coke.

Lawrence's friends were dealers when he was attending school,

After adaptation set in, Lawrence started thinking selling was cool.

One night Lawrence and his friends all went to a party,

They influenced him to take some coke in the parking lot of Hardee's.

Crack was a parasite to Lawrence, he instantly became hooked;

When money was low, coke made him become a crook.

Once Lawrence became addicted, his so-called friends ditched him,

Blinded by crack so strong to this point where he didn't even miss them.

Crack was his best friend for a very long time,

Until police found two rocks on him, went to jail, and paid a nice

**Corey Dixon**

fat fine.

Over the years reality and jail definitely got him straight,

Lawrence could never return to his original state.

While in jail, Lawrence found God and turned his life around,

He's definitely seen low points, being on the same level as the ground.

Lawrence now speaks out against drugs and pure pressure,

He also conducts seminars and youth lectures.

Lawrence is now in his mid-forties and walks with a cane,

He used so much till his nerves sometimes coordinate with his brain.

# The Causes of a Misrouted Foundation

Why are so many young adults and teens so confused?

Is it because they overloaded their brained with the wrong things and became mentally abused, warped?

Is it because of the visual images seen in real life and TV?

Or the influence that comes from watching too much entertainment and types of trends in society?

Is it because of music videos projecting this certain image or style of being cool?

But even some of the entertainers will say those images aren't their lifestyle 24/7, so how come the youth are being fooled?

Is it hearing songs about being dope boys etc. and seeing them locally in the streets?

Always putting shoes on their cars and Jays on their feet?


Now it could be that the blind are leading the blind without any hesitation,

Is it because no one deposited teachings in these kids to where they can build a foundation?

**Corey Dixon**

Is it because kids are having kids,

And they figure it's okay to follow the same broken pattern the parents did like a broken fig?


Maybe it's because the new babysitter is the TV and video games

While the parents are off doing their own individual thang.


Kids are ripe (mentally) and dangerous if they are alone with 100% of control,

That's how the majority get caught up in the stuff by the time they get old.


Now, as for parents, you have to build your kid's foundation, show them love and an adequate amount of time,

And as your child develops, you will see your child's light shine.

# Mentality

What's the setting of your mentality?

Is it on point, or three seconds away from a casualty?

Your mind is the source of it all

That decides the man between mice and others that fall.

Have you ever changed and looked at your mental filter,

Would it be good if someone looked at your inners?

Your mindset determines your outcome,

Will your results be a large or just a small lump sum?

Your mind is a mental stage for your actions,

Are you doing God's work or obtaining personal satisfaction?

If your mind is destroyed you're already wasted,

Everything else follows suit and becomes alienated.

Is the ghetto mind the best way to go?

## Corey Dixon

How many jobs can you obtain with that mindset, though?

One mindset equals one distinctive way,

There are a million choices out there, how can you relate?

Your mind set can be like the Pokémon theme, you have to get them all;

If you applied them right, you'll walk instead of crawl.

Your mind has to remain true to who you are,

Will your current mindset shine in life just like a star?

The mind is like a flower, it needs nutrient to grow;

The flower produces seeds, and the finish product will show.

Your capacity should be limitless while the sky should be your mark,

If you stop learning, your mentality could fall apart.

# Job Security

Hey, do you remember back in the past
When jobs had security that would actually last?

Back then you could get one good job without changing gears,
Mixed with excellent benefits that didn't devalue over the years;

In that time you, could work and save to retire.
Now companies make up things on people to keep cost down and fired.

The work industry in some areas has turned from better to worse,
Now companies are just like the gift and the curse.

'Cause you need a job to create money to buy a few things,
This time of day people get laid off as if they are nothing.

Most companies now are about the major buck,
Treating their employees with low morale, then become bankrupt.

For me, I've encountered three layoffs, all consecutive,
Heard the bad news from all the top executives,

**Corey Dixon**

Saying, We wish you luck, but you have to go;
All you can do then is get your stuff and move to the next show.

From experience, don't ever put too much trust in your job,
All you have to do is put your trust in God.

Companies look at you as another space,
Always learn the facts about the job and always know your place.

If you have security on your job now, it may come with certain stipulations,
Like higher copay with little-to-no vacation.

On the surface they say, Put your money in the 401k!
But we penalize you on it if you take some out today.

Today's time job security is harder to keep, like changing clothes everyday,
Man, this job industry is rough, but it's a game we all must play.

# Fear

Did you know fear is not a quality of God's?

Even though you may not know that or think it sure sounded odd,

Who would want to be scared of everything they do?

You will feel like being rung through a ringer not knowing who is here.

Having fear in you means that you can't focus,

You might as well be out there 'cause you sure will be hopeless.

Having too much fear you will be scared of yourself

And become your own enemy till your death.


Fear is what stops people to succeed,

You're better off having a bad quality like greed.


Too much fear will certainly drive you crazy,

You won't be able to do nothing and just become lazy.


Fear means you are lacking confidence,

Just believe in yourself and know you can be great like a king that has a trident.

**Corey Dixon**

If you need help, start off with something small then build your way on up

Till you gain faith in yourself, then you can never get enough.

So with this poem I hope you can hear

That this trait shouldn't reside in you the quality fear.

# Goal

A man with a plan is a man with a goal,
He's planning on reaching that goal before he gets old.

Always have some kind of goal set up and in reach
That's attainable in life, positive, and something you can teach.

A goal is saying you have something in life planned for you
Despite what you may be, did, or going through.

A goal is saying you are doing something better than nothing,
That means you're a man with a plan that's going to be about something.

A goal puts you on a task, a specific something, or a chore,
Meaning you want more than what you have that's going to be above the floor.

A goal is meeting something with a specific task
Saying, I'm about something in this world that won't leave me in last.

**Corey Dixon**

A goal is a structure plan

That's saying, One day, I will become the man.

It also means you have something to carry out,

And it says you have to make sure you're not in the land of doubt.

A goal is saying you have something you want to accomplish,

No need to worry or fear 'cause you actually can do this.

A goal is ways to others saying you have a plan,

And this is something that concerns you that you'll become a man.

**Various Shades of Poetry**

# Spirit vs. Flesh

A guy had two conversations over the phone today. One was with the spirit, the other with the flesh. Who was going to come out being the best? And who was he going to pledge his allegiance with?

Conversation One: The Spirit

I had some questions with you and wanted to know the answer today,

So I'm going begin now, okay? Go ahead.

So I was wondering what I get if I sided with you.

You get to live here in heaven for an eternity, and we reside above the big blue.

So what is your record like?

Well, my friend, we have never lost since Earth existed and will not lose, little tyke.

So what about eternity?

Well, it's a piece of me in you, and that's all dependent on who you choose, are you feeling me?

**Corey Dixon**

What about the blessing then? Well, nothing is free; it comes with hard work,

You may have to work a little bit, may even have to shovel some dirt.

That's cool, the guy responded, Nothing comes free,

The only thing free is getting stung by a bumblebee.

But if you side with us, you have angels and etc. and will get bless.

Well, that's tight right there, that would take away some of the stress.

All you have to do is follow the Bible's pattern there on Earth,

And you shall see what it is really like here and heaven, and will experience pure bliss, and know our heavenly worth.

Well, that's cool right there, I'm down for that,

He says, Thanks for helping me out with those questions, Pat.

Well, I know you have questions with the Flesh too,

Just watch out for yourself 'cause he going to try to influence you to be a part of his crew.

**Various Shades of Poetry**

Conversation Two: The Flesh

The man says I have some questions to ask.

Flesh says, No problem, I'll answer them in a flash.

He says, What do I get if I side with you?

Flesh replies, You get money, fame, wealth, and cars sitting on 22s.

The guy says, Now that's good living and sure would be nice,

I know nothing is free, so it has to come with a price.

Flesh says, You're a smart man, I must admit;

Flesh knew if he lied about the truth, the guy would be chilling in a pit.

The man asks, What's your record like? Flesh says, We got one big battle that we won;

The one he was referring to was the Resurrection of Jesus Christ, God's only son.

Flesh goes on and says, We can give you the best at what the world has to offer,

We can give you trips, drugs, chicks, and guys, right on a saucer.

**Corey Dixon**

The man says, Whoa, whoa, whoa, I don't get down like that;

Flesh laughs and says, That's cool, let's get back on track.

The guy probes on and says, Well, how long the blessings take? Flesh says, Oh yeah, my man, they come real fast;

But he forgot to tell him that they won't last.

Flesh says, All you have to do is sign on the dotted line,

We can get you enrolled today, but your soul is mine;

Man, I don't know about my soul, and that's on the real;

Flash says, Come on, my man, you know you got the best of the deal.

The guy says, Well, what about eternity? Flesh says, You will have all types of fun;

Flesh didn't tell him that it resides under the sun.

Flesh continues, Man, I got people, too;

Didn't tell him the same people that will torture him will be a part of his crew.

Flesh says, I know you already talked with the Spirit,

What he told you was a bunch of lies, dude, don't even try to hear it.

By this time Flesh was antsy and mad,

That's when the phone hung up and, boy, was I glad.

After getting off the phone, he thought with extra precision,

He knew it was time to make a decision.

So he called both back to say,

Guys, I thought about it and chosen the Spirit, end this very day.

Corey Dixon

# Fridays

Adults and kids like this day

'Cause kids got two days off from school, and adults most likely got paid.

For kids, they happy 'cause they got two days off,

Some adults have money in their pocket from working, now they're off.

Friday is a busy day

'Cause a lot of activities go off on that day, like a parade,

'Specially for adults, they definitely like pay day,

Adults are happy, like saying Hip hop hooray!

Kids love it 'cause it brings them to the weekend,

Which means no school, most time no getting up early, so let the cartoons begin.

And for some adults, they happy 'cause it's one more day closer to the clubs,

And they can relax and do nothing; maybe the boyfriend or girlfriend will celebrate that with a back rub.

Some people have the weekend off

To do nothing but go grocery shopping right there around the shopping plaza or lofts.

For most people, Fridays are not as stressful,

As long as you follow rules and just obey laws and be respectful.

I know Fridays are good 'cause three movies was made about it

By Ice Cube and Chris Tucker; they were alright with me for doing it.

So there's one question that is left:

What will your Friday contain for?

# This Poem is Like a Commercial

Why do you feel down all the time?

Do you need help with some things?

Do you know what your purpose in life is for?

Do you know what the Bible means?

Do you read your Bible or know what it's about?

Are you one of the people that harbors a lot of doubt?

Are you one of the people that harbors fear,

Even when someone's far away from you or near?

Do you know what rules and lists you supposed to follow?

Are you missing something in life that makes you feel hollow?

Do you know who you supposed to serve?

Are you wondering why everything is so easy to get on your nerves?

Well, I have two answers that can help you out with all you need,

That God and Jesus are there for you and to help you always, and they never sleep either!

Isn't that good to know? There's someone watching you all the time to make you look and feel extremely easier.

So when you think you are down and out,

**Corey Dixon**

God and Jesus help you with absolutely no doubt

Even if you feel shaken up like you're in a storm,

Are you shaking like you woke up by an alarm?

Just know you always have help

On any side of you till the last breath,

All the way till your death.

That's good right there to know you are never left,

I'm glad I got two supernatural bodyguards

That also know everything I do and how to play my cards.

And they watch out to like I'm heavily have two guards

That are always ready if anything starts.

# Chapter 3

Corey Dixon

# Basketball

If I had to pick one sport out of them all,

My selection definitely be the game of basketball.

The game is universal; you can go play anywhere and say,

Go get a team of five together and a ball and begin to play.

All over the world people remember great names like Jordan, Bird, Erving, and Russell,

All of them are in the Hall of Fame for their outstanding play and excellent hustle.

Over the years the game has made legendary events like the EBC and the Rucker's,

I'm glad I didn't play with Stockton and Malone when they wore those short hip huggers.

Now the game has changed with an arsenal of moves,

Like the crossover, hesitation, and spin that would give the defender the blues.

Don't forget about the no-look pass and the mid-jump assists,

Magic Johnson was the man who could throw the ball to you if you was in his midst.

When dunking on someone, you always get mad respect,

As well if you hit a buzzer beater that goes straight through the net.

If you want to become good, you have to train and sweat,

Nothing in this game comes easy, on that you can beat.

Can you believe how this round ball can take you far,

From scholarships, shoe deals, NBA, big house, luxury car.

So a great deal of respect is due and goes out to Mr. Naismith

'Cause if it weren't for his bright ideas, what sport would we have to play with?

**Various Shades of Poetry**

# Teen Years

Do you remember your teen years,

When things were a lot simpler compared to your adult years?

Once you reached high school it was about how you dress and look,

All you had to do is go to class and carry a few books.

Your parents at the time wanted you to stay in school,

If you played a sport you were popular and considered cool.

On top of that, you even had a summer break

To relax and do nothing but watch TV and eat grapes.

Most people thought they were grown by the time they reached sixteen,

That was the official age for a teenager, you felt so esteemed;

Now you were eligible to drive,

Most teens were geared by this, of having the freedom to ride.

By this time a lot of teens were introduced to a working job

So they can purchase their own clothes instead of doing nothing

**Corey Dixon**

like a slob.

Some teens would do things and sneak around their parents' backs,
Just to get caught up by a left-out fact.

Other teens were stereotyped for doing wrong,
If they got caught they were still punished, even while they are now grown.

What about all those times of talking on the phone,
You rarely had a dull moment of being alone.

And who can forget the big winter ball,
Where most schools would have dances in the fall.
The teen years definitely included a lot of fun,
Adulthood carries more responsibility when you become one.

**Various Shades of Poetry**

# Story and Aftermath of Cain and Abel

Adam and Eve had two sons named Abel and Cain,

Who knew that his anger would had driven him to slain?

Abel brought the Lord an offering out of his flock,

He made sure to bring the firstborn out of his stock.

Cain also brought an offering, but his was denied;

Cain was sad and depressed, all he could do was sigh.

The Lord told Cain "If you do well, your offering will be accepted,

But you master it, otherwise it will be rejected."

After the conversation with God Cain's heart still harbored with jealously,

He would kill his brother in the field to make a decision so recklessly.

God already knew Cain killed another,

**Corey Dixon**

God asked Cain, "Where is Abel, your brother?"

God told Cain "When you till the ground, it will no longer yield its power;"

Cain shall now be a wanderer of Earth, I know he felt sour.

This is what happens once envy settles in,

After killing his own brother, he still didn't accomplish anything.

# Lifesaver

A man had a friend named Laureen,

She was the smartest labrador you've ever seen.

The man was visually impaired,

Laureen was always there for him; she was the only one who cared.

Laureen would help him through doors,

She would help him out with a variety of chores.

They had a bond stronger than any relationship,

He would sit back with his soda as Laureen would go grab the chips.

One day the man left his window up and drifted to sleep,

Laureen always watched him, she took care of her peeps.

Hours later it began to rain,

Water began to enter through the window as it bounced off the pane.

**Corey Dixon**

The water eventually formed a puddle,
It reached an electrical cord, which meant trouble.

We know water and electricity don't mix,
Laureen hurried to find a quick fix.

Laureen got a whiff of it and jumped right up,
But Laureen barking frantically was just not enough.

Laureen went into panic mode as she ran around,
She dragged the man from the bed right to the ground.

Laureen kept dragging until she got him to the door,
By that time the man had collapsed right to the floor.

The neighbor saw smoke, rushed to give CPR just to breathe,
Once he came to, Laureen was quite relieved.
Firefighters arrived, but the house was completely ablaze,
The man said, Thank God, for Laureen was surely brave.

# A Torn Kingdom

Saul was forty years old when he began his regime
But couldn't follow God's orders through Samuel that was straight and clean.

After the third Saul did evil in the Lord's sight,
Samuel told him his kingdom would be torn and he would lose his might.

You see, Saul thought he could just be forgiven with a repent,
Saul thought the Lord was easy, as if He could be bent.

God told Samuel to go see Jesse of Bethlehem to find his new king,
Samuel went on his quest to find his new anointing.

The Lord told Samuel "Don't look at the appearance or the statue of height,"
Because the Lord looks inward at the heart of might.

Samuel held the oil over six of Jesse's sons before they called over David,
As Samuel held the oil over his head, it began to anoint him as

**Corey Dixon**

God's favorite.

The Lord troubled Saul with an evil spirit,
Saul requested for David for his skills on the lyre so he could hear it.

David came to play for Saul as he became refreshed,
David's journey just began as he passed his test.

After this time Israel was at war with the Philistines,
The leader was Goliath, who's of Gath, whose armor was one of a kind.

Goliath shouted, "If someone kills me, the people will be yours,
If we win, you will become our slaves to do chores."

Israel was afraid when they heard this,
Everyone but David was definitely nervous.

David knew God had his back so he had no fear,
He would keep his faith because victory was near.

David went to battle with a sling and stones,
He definitely was anointed with courage of someone grown.

## Various Shades of Poetry

Goliath saw David and laughed out loud,

You know what happened, what happens when people become proud.

David ran up and hit Goliath in the head with a stone,

Goliath laid lifeless as he was left all alone.

# Egypt

Egyptians enslaved Israelites because they saw their true potential,

So the new king broke that up because of their strong credentials.

Pharaoh was the king that tried to make Israel feel inferior,

But Pharaoh didn't know who he was up against, messing with Moses' superiors.

Everything changed once Moses met the Lord at the burning bush,

From that point on Moses would gain confidence and no longer stay shushed.


This is one of the most famous statements everyone knows,

When Moses told old pharaoh to Let my people go.

Every time Moses and Aaron performed miracles by God, the devil tried to duplicate,

The authority of God always showed rank when the devil's miracles were eradicated.


As time went on more and more miracles were performed,

## Various Shades of Poetry

The one that hurt Pharaoh was the Lord's Passover, killing Egypt's firstborn.

Four hundred thirty years, the Israelites were slaves,

God's on their side and remains to keeps promises always.

The Israelites left Egypt while Pharaoh pursued to attack,

Just like an Indian giver, get mad, always trying to take things back.

God then opened the waters of the Red Sea,

Pharaoh tried to cross, all of them were captured in the waters, not one left in the vicinity.

## Miracle

A man was just diagnosed with cancer,

He didn't know what to do, but he knew who to go to for the answer.

He thought, How can this be? He's forty-three, healthy, wealthy, and a successful business man

Who had it all together, plus a wife and a son that was named Dan.

The next couple of days in his house were strife

Because he didn't know how to discuss the cancer with his wife.

He finally broke down and told her what happen,

She digested the information, and "Lets called on the captain."

He told her that he was scheduled next week for an appointment,

They both did daily spiritual anointments.

Although you would have thought that Dan Sr. was going to be

**Various Shades of Poetry**

depressed and down,

He kept his confidence and head up like royalty, as if he wore a crown.

Six days later, it was time to go back and see the doc,

The appointment was bright and early, right at 10 'o clock.

Dan told his wife he would see her when she came back home,

If anything is up, he will notify her by phone.

Once he arrived, the doc did various tests,

Over his whole body, especially in his chest.

The doctor reviewed the cancer test, and they came back negative,

Dan says, "Thank you, God, for being receptive."

The doctor says, "Did you do something different since the last time you came?"

Dan says, "I did, I claimed authority over that cancer in Jesus' name."

**Corey Dixon**

# Scenic Tour

A boy was with his dad; he was the happiest little man,
He just found out that they were going to Disneyland!

The father promised the boy that they will be on their way,
However they will have some stops to make on their long journey.

The next day, the dynamic duo left in the morning,
The boy was consumed by sleep and began snoring.

Hours later the boy arose from his sleep and said, "Are we there yet, Pops?"
"No, not yet, son, we still have to make more stops."

The boy was sitting impatiently and bored out of his mind
As he looked out the window and stared off into the sunshine.

The end of the day came, and they approached a hotel in a town,
The dad looked at the boy's face and saw a frown.

Dad knew his son was restless and knew what he was going through,

**Various Shades of Poetry**

Dad decided to pick his son's spirits up to keep him away from feeling the blues.

Dad said to his son what he needed to hear,

Once again the little boy was revitalized with an excitement of cheers.

A couple days went by and it was the same routine,

The little boy was moving faster than ants running up his spleen.

Once they arrived, Dad was extremely glad,

The boy was seeing eye to eye with Pops 'cause he sure was mad.

Son said, "Dad, we drove around for a bunch of days,

But I haven't seen any Disney sign or any places to play."

The boy continued to talk and didn't want to be refused,

All Dad wanted to do was tell him to look up at the Disney sign so the bomb could be diffused.

Dad said, "Well, son, I promised you all along the way,

I see you didn't believe that everything would be okay."

"Son, all you had to do is wait and believe,

**Corey Dixon**

Open the door and you will finally see."

As they approached the front, the boy saw the Disney sign and became happy,

He still has the picture to this day that he took with Mr. Mickey and his Pappy.

# Chapter 4

**Corey Dixon**

# My Five (B-Ball)

If I had to pick five people, my five would be—

At starting center, Bill Russell, always was known for his outstanding play and his hustle;

My fourth would be tiny Tim Duncan 'cause the man got skills, plus a couple NBA rings;

My third guy would be Julius Erving 'cause he was cool in his era and no one could stop him;

My second guy would be none other than the greatest player in the universe, Mr. Michael Jordan himself;

The last guy would be today's runner up, Mr. LeBron James, the today's Michael Jordan, 'cause he's dominating and didn't go to college and producing better than folks that went to college.

## Busch Stadium

I remember the good ole years I worked at Busch Stadium,

When everyone wanted to play against them.

When I worked there, they had greats like Ozzie Smith and Big Mac,

Who is now Albert Pujols with a big bat.

I remember catching the public transportation up there and the MetroLink,

The Cardinals always wore red, never wore the color pink

Especially selling those high-priced sodas was definitely a lot,

But when you in the heat, they sure hit the spot.

And then stars like Mark McGwire breaking the home run record,

People would go crazy there, waving a flag around as Big Mac to the flag to be checkered.

I remember all the mullah I used to make,

That's how I upgraded my shoe game to Jordans I would say.

**Corey Dixon**

I gave Busch Stadium three or four years of good service,

Now I make a little more than that now while some are getting nervous.

But I remember hot working the top of the seats at the old Busch,

At the old Busch them where some high seats where no one could hear you say shush!

But those was the years,

The good ole memories no one can take, so that deserves a cheer!

Go Cards!

# Drama

Everybody knows at least one person that always loves drama,

I don't know if it's natural, or did it come from their daddy or mama?

Drama people give it their best

To attract as many people as possible up in their mess,

Drama people have to add gas to the fire to stir up a mix,

They act as if they have a mental disease that can't be fix.

Drama is nothing but negativity's first cousin,

It's like a muffin with yeast, it gets bigger once heat is applied in the oven.

People with this trait have either a lot of friends or a lot of enemies,

Saying trigger words to get everyone riled up in the vicinity.

Like bragging to friends how they told someone off as if it's an achievement,

**Corey Dixon**

Some people are so good at drama their stories always carry around extra accouterment.


When they speak, don't go back and forwards, fight or verbally diss 'em,

To overcome you simply have to resist them.


Drama is sometimes initiated or started with force,

Just remember drama and anything else can be defeated if you supply the solution to the source.

# Brother (Skit)

Now I'm walking down the store to my car in a lot,

And a brother approaches me, saying, "I've got some CD's to sell on the spot."

"Five for ten will get you in,"

I'm saying to myself, Not this again!

So I listen to the thirty-sec spiel,

He says, "Support ya Black brother, and I will throw an extra CD in for the deal."

I put the CD in,

And this is how this story begins.

Now I'm down for ethnicity, my brother,

Only thing separates us is a different mother.

## Corey Dixon

But what happen is that he's undercover to himself while presenting a mirage to others,

Including all skins of life, especially his African American brother.

Now I'm his hustle to try to make some money,

But selling me CD's with nothing on them is way past not funny.

Why do some of us complain about not spending dollars in the hood?

The quality of the product is either false, fake, or ten times away from being good.

When I know there are exceptions to every rule,

So to categorize everybody would entail the mentality of a fool.

Another thing I know for a fact,

The same politician who wants you to spend money in the hood won't have your back.

So as I come to a close I just wanted to say,

You get what you pay for; I now have some CD's to give away.

# Deepest Sympathy

When someone close to us passes, we often wonder why,

Leaving us with feelings to make us want to cry.

Most times we don't know the specific reason,

Everything has a time structure that falls in to the appropriate season.

No one likes to deal with losing a family member,

All you can do is extract the good out of it and remember…

Remember the fun times that you spent together,

Remember the event that brought you two closer when standing against the weather.

I know right now you may endure some sorrow,

The long run carries light that will shine bright on your tomorrow.

Everything in life unfortunately has to end,

This is where the legacy of the loved one lives through you as another chapter of your life begins.

**Corey Dixon**

Call on God when in need, to give you the might and strength;

We continue to keep you in our heart and prayers in the midst of your absence.

We send condolences to you and your family through the power of a pen,

Your family will also help you get back to the stages of a grin.

# A Past Hobby

I remember the past thing for me to do was basketball card collecting,

That was something I was proud of; in a conversation I was so reaccepting;

Especially when you got a pack of cards that had Michael Jordon in it,

You thought you were on top of the world, then it was something you could admire to

finish;

Especially to have a hot rookie card like a Kevin Garnet,

You might think if you played ball, things would go straight in the net.

But I sure did rack up a lot of cards then,

I'm pretty sure they could be worth some money now, and I know they are worth more than a pen.

But I even used to go card collecting with an adult,

We used to be a one-and-two-man combo, like we was in a cult.

**Corey Dixon**

I almost now want to get a card book and check them out,
Who knows now? You might get big money for them, may even pull some clout.

But I finally, after about five years, upgraded to video games,
But back then card collecting was a sport in a sense, never lame.
So for all you card collectors, keep it up,
Don't ever stop till you got enough.

# Drugs

D – To me really stands for demonic;

R – Is to be in a resistance from the truth;

U – Would be to hide underneath an umbrella for cover 'cause no one will do it in front of a police;

G – Would be making you guessing and gullible 'cause it will make you feel different;

S – This is a temporary thing, it's really not satisfying.

Corey Dixon

# The Power of Words

Did you know the power of life and death comes in the power of the tongue?

That's power right there compared to none.

Out of the abundance of the heart the mouth will speak,

I hope you know this already so this message won't become bleak.

A lot of power compared through the power of mouth,

That performs and utters words and sound that hopefully won't take you south.

Words can either make you build up or tear you apart,

Don't even let me begin with those words, or I will have to start.

In the things called words utters an existence,

So be careful between all words and the persistence.

Words could make you or break you,

Just like a game of B-ball they could actually take you.

Words are something people don't know that is a powerful thing,

Do you hear what I am saying or know what I mean?

**Various Shades of Poetry**

So next time think about what comes out of your mouth,

Just don't act like a bird when it gets cold, don't go and run or fly south.

Corey Dixon

# Fast Small World, Pt 1

Monique was a girl who loved to live fast,

Never thought about consequences, if she should crash.

Monique could get any dude she wanted to spend money on her with tight game,

With stats like hers, she qualified for the player's hall of fame.

Monique would only talk to suga' daddies, hustlers, and ballers,

If she gave the number out, she definitely got callers!

She went to the clubs, parades, and any type of festivities,

Changing guys to her was like another activity.

Monique had a rep as a man abuser,

Didn't matter to the guys, they would still choose her.

Monique received it all: trips, clothes, cars, tickets to the concerts and shows,

Chicks hated on her house 'cause Monique was who they chose.

Monique, it's not her fault that some man was stupid,

### Various Shades of Poetry

Didn't realize one day she would meet her cupid.

Monique was trying to call her girls to go down on an event on Natural Bridge,

To see what ballers that would be there stunting in the cars with Lamborghini doors that opened like coffee lids.

So they went on down with the tightest clothes on to grab the male's attention,

To find a new baller to take them shopping, and misuse was their true intentions.

When they arrived, they had a lot of success,

Monique only wanted the best of the best.

Ten minutes in, Monique saw a guy in a new Hummer 3 riding on twenty-eights,

The only person down there with that size rims, Monique dreamed of money falling right into her plate.

So Monique went to cross the street in front of the guy to get him to stop,

As she walked by, he said, "What's up, little mama? You want to go somewhere with me, and we can kickback and shop."

# Corey Dixon

She said, "Sure. My girls with me, can they come, too?"

He said, "My truck could fit you and the whole crew."

Monique's friend Parris declined the offer, but put up some resistance,

Parris stayed behind till she got herself a baller, she was more persistent.

Three of Monique's friends left while the other stayed,

They agreed to check on each other to make sure they were okay.

Monique said, "What's your name?" He said Gregory James,

Monique was always like that, she had no shame.

They went to the Cheesecake Factory in the mall,

As Greg promised, he took care of them all.

Monique and Greg hit it off big that day and talked for hours,

Greg dropped her friends off and invited her back to the La Towers.

They went back and chilled for a moment or two,

She woke up in the morning to the balcony view.

## Various Shades of Poetry

To find out what happened, I would give you clues,

You will see in the sequel, part two…

Corey Dixon

# Weed

See, I'm going to break down what you think you need,

I'm going to break it down for you what young people crave, and that's weed.

Did you know weed is an addictive drug that seems like you have to have it?

Weed is also a parasite that would turn you into a misfit.

What happens is, long term, it turns you into an addict,

Then weed will make you into a savage.

You see, weed will make you do some things that are pointless

Till it will turn you to a point where you will become jointless.

Then weed will move up till it becomes your god,

You will make that your first priority; that definitely is odd.

Then you will become a crook, if you stay with someone, to steal for cash,

Others will then see that, and then start to laugh.

## Various Shades of Poetry

Then when you can't have it, weed would make you do obscene things

Just to smoke on it, like get inside your head, then your soul, to eat you alive;

Then you may have repercussions to where you think you can't survive.

Weed also is more of a threat than cigarettes, it also bring you quicker to cancer,

I believe one joint is like ten cigarettes; it would kill you quicker than a vital disease,

You never will feel at ease.


Man, I'm cool on that joint, then like saying, Negro please.

If you need help, just ask Jesus to make you feel right at ease,

All you have to do is please have faith or confidence, and really believe.

Corey Dixon

# Too Good to Be True

I started off with my routine I do every day,

But I stop by a store to buy a lottery ticket. and decided to play.

Hours later, I took a break while I was at work,

Complaining to my buddies on the gig about our supervisor because he's a consistent jerk.

I said if I can leave this job, I sure wouldn't miss it,

As I told them I'm going to win some money with this lottery ticket.

After they said their whatevers, we all went away,

I knew this would be my very lucky day.

The next break came and we seen the lottery number roll across the TV;

I look at my ticket, and they matched up all perfectly.

I said "I won, I won" emphatically, and withdrew from my mouth was spit;

Everyone else with me covered up their faces because it was a direct hit.

So as I continued to throw a ruckus and had everyone's attention,

I made sure I told everyone what they can do with this position.

While all of this was happening right on the scene,

I was greeted with drool on my face and an alarm clock, and said, I can't believe it, this was a dream?

After realizing this was a dream, I was deeply hurt;

All I can do now is sighing and get ready for work.

Corey Dixon

# Lacking

I don't know if something is wrong with your mackin',

But you don't seem right, but you're definitely lacking.

See, lacking means you didn't get enough,

Just don't get fed up, like blowup and erupt!

Lacking means you don't have enough of something;

We don't know what it is, but it's something you're definitely missing.

Lacking is also a withdrawal of something

When most times it's all or nothing, but it's definitely something,

Meaning your all together physically, but something's missing.

Just find it, fix it, but don't get mad like a snake and start hissing.

Just work on that area till the situation decreases,

It can be you, your uncle, or you nieces.

# Various Shades of Poetry

But when something's lacking, you're not all together,

And that's the element you need to arm you against, per say, the weather.

Lacking definitely shows a apart of you may be weak,

Just fix that area 'cause no one likes leaks.

But to add to the leak just add some more,

To catch you up on something like you buy something at a store.

Lacking means basically you're really without,

Just kill it there, don't let it grow bigger, to like having doubts.

## Fast Small World, Pt 2

Gregory Curtis James lived in the La Towers,

His place, the dungeon, is where his victims were being devoured.

Greg owned a lot of realty and shops,

Owned a few cars, some were dropped.

Some chicks wanted him because of what he had,

He would do them in once they were at his pad.

Greg was six-one, 220, with muscles showing in his back,

He would always have in his platinum rack.

Greg had a rep of womanizer, but chicks didn't care,

It was cool as long as he paid a few bills and for their weaved in hair.

Greg went to the doc monthly to give a blood sample,

He was a sex addicted, his list was ample.

**Various Shades of Poetry**

Three weeks before the event, Greg went out to the pub

To see if he was taking a victim home from the club.

Greg saw an attractive girl with a nice bottle shape,

Other males were conducting themselves like apes.

Greg told his guys that was who he was about to get,

He said, Certainty that's who I am leaving with!

Thirty minutes went by, the lady walked right past;

He grabbed her hand smooth but fast.

Greg said, You look like someone I can cherish,

What's your name, baby?" She said Parris.

Parris was yellow, just like the drink Sunny D;

Guys would never focus on her, but always her booty.

Greg could tell Parris was real smooth,

He adapted to her first, then made his move.

He asked if she knew about the event;

## Corey Dixon

What event? He said, "You must be sleeping in a tent."

Parris said, "What are you talking about?"
"It's a Black get together where I can bring my new Hummer out."

She went back with him, while they did the routine;
Next morning she was laid right against his spleen.

Parris said, "By the way, I forgot your name;"
"Oh yeah, Parris, they call me Curtis James."

Once Parris left, the game had changed;
Let me explain to you why this chick was insane.

Parris was promiscuous, loved to have one night stands,
She contracted herpes by another unknown man.

Parris was passing it on to males in her vicinity,
She changed her look to maintain her identity.

Before the event, Greg purchased the Hummer;
He would be killing 'em with them twenty-eights this summer.

**Various Shades of Poetry**

Next day Greg was driving down the event on Natural Bridge to a friend's picnic

But was stopped by a fine chick that was fine and thick.

Greg said, "What's up, little mama? You want to kick back and shop?"

Parris saw the Hummer, and her mouth dropped.

She didn't know if he found out or not,

She was scared to her stomach, was tying itself in knots.

Greg thought he knew her but couldn't tell by the look,

Parris tried to stay calm but was shaking like a crook.

Now we're going to fast-forward and fill in the blanks,

This story about to get ugly, might even stank.

Monique was chilling at Greg's after eating the food,

She slipped on something more comfortable to enjoy the mood.

Ten minutes later they were sexually subdued,

They did their thing all the way till the morning dew.

## Corey Dixon

A week passed, it was time for Monique and a visit with the doc;

That's when they received news, it put them to shock.

Doc said, "Greg, you tested positive for herpes;"

Greg got on the phone and called Monique urgently.

Monique's doc went to do a pap smear,

But seen a foggy color in her urine that was unclear;

Doc said, "Monique, you tested positive for a herpes disease,"

She dialed Greg's number swiftly.

Greg and Monique called each other at the same time,

Trying to figure out who was at fault, was it hers or mine?

After arguing back and forth for a long while,

They decided to work together instead of acting like a child.

Greg said, "I slept with two people this month, you and this woman named Parris;"

Monique said, "Does her last name begin with the letter F, as in Ferris?"

## Various Shades of Poetry

"I don't know, it was a one night stand;

As a matter of fact, I have the woman's number right in my hand."

Monique started thinking back to the event, to put the pieces back together to the puzzle;

She growled furiously as if she had on a muzzle.

Greg said, "Last month I was disease free,

If it wasn't you, then she's the only one it could be."

Monique knew if Greg called he wouldn't get her to stumble,

She called them on three-way to get her to fumble.

Monique asked Parris," "Do you know a guy named Curtis?"

"Don't mess with him though, girl, he's really worthless."

Greg got mad and erupted on the phone;

Parris responded angrily, but her cover was blown.

Parris said, "I give back to males so they can be like me;"

Monique heard those words and broke down instantly.

**Corey Dixon**

Greg and Monique called the police; they took Parris to jail,

She was charged with endangerment to others as her plans were derailed.

You can see Greg and Monique

Doing Valtrex commercials every week.

# Hating

You know someone in the world is always hating,

I think that they must be mad, need help, are always wanted to be participating.

Haters always want to hold you back or see you struggling,

So you want to get ahead of them or to see them struggling.

Hating is whether to do something to you or spread rumors,

They won't be success, feel successful, till they start to grow tumors.

Hating indeed isn't good for the heart

'Cause you'll be cool as long as you be not with, more like apart.

Haters want to hate 'cause they can't see you have success,

They think haters hate just to give you turmoil, the best.

Haters are like a pain in your side

'Cause they want to get at you and try to take your pride.

Haters never take a day off, always doing what they do;

**Corey Dixon**

All you trying to do is tell them to stay away from you.

Haters hate, they don't need a crew;
All they want to do is get at you.

They really don't have an explanation,
So they do what they do best, and that's start hating.

And no! They will never leave you alone
Until they mess you up or get you out your zone.

Haters are like a rash, they want to get inside,
They want to stick to you and don't want you to break away with a stride.

It's something wrong with haters because they want to see you down
At all cost, like do stuff to you when you are not doing nothing for yourself,
to make you the clown.

So my advice, keep doing what you doing
'Cause somebody will hate regardless, so keep pursuing.

**Various Shades of Poetry**

But for real I'm displaying how society can really be;

People, whatever you do, do it safe or this can become your reality.

Corey Dixon

# Don't Be Friends with the Enemy

Now, don't be friends with the enemy
'Cause they trying to catch you right up in your vicinity.

They want to invite you to be, act like you're buddy-buddy,
Just to draw you in till you get trapped, just like you're in some water feeling floody.

Now, the Bible says to forgive your enemies;
You can do that, but you don't have to let them trap you in their vicinity.

You just forgive them and leave them alone,
And don't harbor hate inside yourself to find you are who's wrong.

'Cause by being friends with the enemy or used-to-be enemy,
They can find flaws on you to hold you up from small to plenty;

And then they show signs of fakeness
When they show you they have a character of flakiness.

**Various Shades of Poetry**

'Cause a clouded head makes bad decisions,

And you don't want to trap yourself up in it, like revisiting.


That's why it's so important to stay far away,

'Cause you don't want to be carried up in their mess today!


You just trying to keep the peace

By not really dealing with them; so no more you and me.


'Cause if they are really supposed to be your cordial friends, they won't take you to court

On things like phony stuff, fake lies about some child support.


And you ain't gave them no recognition of being that way or doing so,

So they're just using up a lot of air in themselves; so just tell them to sit down and begin to blow.

**Corey Dixon**

# Graduating

When you graduate that moves you up one

Till you get finished with whatever you're trying to start or finish or done;

Graduating is a time of celebration

That's pretty much understood across the nation;

Nowadays you get a big show

Letting people know you don't have far to go;

It basically means one task is done and you're on to the next one,

Keep it up or going till you have a collection like a lump sum.


Because graduating shows a sign of finishing,

And nothing's lost or left behind, like something is diminishing.


You step across a platform letting people know you're passing on to the next task,

And you keep going till you reach the last of the last.

## Various Shades of Poetry

Some family members and friend come out to show support,

They are all there cheering you or like it's your last resort.

So keep up the good work

'Cause it's a celebrating function and shows you're doing something and not playing with dirt;

So when it's your time to walk around that stage,

Hold your head really high and show that you're brave.

**Corey Dixon**

# Plan

A person is dangerous if they have a plan

Regardless of who it is, man or woman.

A person with a plan shows that you're doing something with your life,

It shows that you're trying to do something, no longer be trifling.

And that shows that you're about something,

That you ain't here using space and doing nothing.

Anyone that has a plan is a dangerous person

Because they're striving towards their mark being better than the original one.

It also shows that you took your thing into consideration,

To achieve it you will feel full of esteem, like you belong as residents to this nation;

## Various Shades of Poetry

It also shows that you have a brain,

And you're worth much more, instead of going crazy and insane.


Whatever you do, make sure you have something that's positive

And do something that will not make you derogative.


So for the folks out there with a real plan,

Strive for excellence and obtaining it to become that man or woman.

**Corey Dixon**

# Lazy

Don't you dislike a person who is lazy?

'Cause they act like they in slow motion, as if they were hazy?

Being lazy is definitely not a good look,

Then people will think as you do nothing, crook.

You get tired messing with lazy folks

'Cause they don't know how to do nothing, just go all day with some, but mope.

They never feel like doing any more;

If they have to, they start to whine, as if it was a chore.

Then you don't want to have nothing to do with them;

If they don't want to do nothing, leave them or just say, Forget it, screw 'em.

You're not going to accomplish nothing being lazy

And then wondering why folks looking at you weird, as if you're crazy.

# Various Shades of Poetry

Laziness should be for a short period of time,

But to me it should be illegal, as if it were a crime.


Nobody likes anyone that's lazy

Because they always feel like something is up, acting shady.


I just hope that it's in and out like a quick fad

Because long term is a germ for them, like pursuing a goal and becoming a grad.


So whatever you do, don't be lazy,

Unless you like for people to look at you crazy.

Corey Dixon

# Automobile

I don't know if you plan to go far,
But in this day and age, you do need a car.

You need a car for things like getting back and forward to work
And to do multiple things in a short amount of time, like various
    tasks like taking something to a drycleaner like a shirt.

Now, with a respectable car you have a little mine of work,
But it gets you from point A, B, C, all in a matter of a small amount of dirt.

Cars take you around to several places
Like work, store, and church to see some familiar faces.

But you do have to worry about high-priced gas,
But you can get from A, B, C; hopefully the high gas won't last.

Now, a car makes things simple,
Easier than a hot date with a girl that doesn't have a pimple.

## Various Shades of Poetry

So with cars get time now 'cause the bi-state may be rough;

And once you get a car, you might fall in love all over again, like you can't get enough;

So thank the inventor for making cars,

That's why sixteen years olds are so happy, 'cause they can drive cars.

**Corey Dixon**

# Pursuing

I don't care what you think you are doing,
Just keep it up, don't quit, keep pursuing.

Pursuing means something you're after, like a task,
So you don't want it to be over without being completed or it will seem real fast.

Pursuing is good 'cause that means you're after something,
And that's always better than doing nothing;
Pursuing means you have something down in mind,
And that's good as long as it don't take up too much of your time;
Pursuing is saying, I'm here for an adventure,
That's good 'cause you could be doing nothing and foaming for some dentures.
Pursuing is also good 'cause that means you're thinking of something to conquer a thing,
Like finishing school or gaining knowledge to get rich and buy some bling-bling.

### Various Shades of Poetry

Pursuing means you're after whatever you have planned,

And as you know, accomplishing it will make you the man or woman.


Pursuing means you're after something you have thought of or dreamed,

Just 'cause you thought of it doesn't mean it's going be as easy as it seemed.


But pursuing something means you have heart,

And nobody can do anything to you to tear that away or apart.

# Paycheck

Do you know one thing that people always respect?

That's the green thing, not weed, but a paycheck;

You never see anyone be mad because they have gotten paid—

Because it is payday, just look around, folks happy anyway;

They're happy 'cause they got a little bit of cash,

Most people have things to do with it, like pay bills with their cash.

So on that day most people are happy

'Cause it's payday for some, like they are far from being crappy.

It's like you're okay 'cause you got a pocketful of money,

And you're off to business and fun and far from a dummy.

Most people are happy and jump for joy like a bunny,

Like when a bunny finds a carrot, I bet to them it tastes yummy.

So a paycheck is a day of action,

Most people feel like they did something that day and they're getting satisfaction.

**Various Shades of Poetry**

So you know what rhymes with intellect,

It's what you're going to do with your paycheck.

But a paycheck is a fun occasion

That's respected for working folk throughout the nation.

## **Dream**

D – Is to be determined after your dream and never lose focus;

R – Realizing your dream can come true, and never lose and be hopeless;

E – Always educate yourself on whatever it is you're trying to accomplish;

A – Ask questions about it if you know someone that's doing what you're pursuing;

M – Make more things that you're trying to do, more moving in that field in whatever you're doing.

# Rhyming vs. Poetry

Both of these different subjects have a lot of things that are the similarity,

So let's talk about them to see why they're different and the other one is unique:

Both of them include some rhyming,

Both of them can do things to make you start shining;

One is different 'cause it may be a hot sixteen,

The other one is not dirty but always being clean;

They are familiar 'cause they be connecting the dots per say;

One can equal big money, or both could make money in a lot,

Both are bringing on different views, making them famous on the spot.

## Corey Dixon

Both of them really have a different setting:

One is making more money than the other one, like who is the one that's netting?

But I'm just going over a few of the facts,

They're both decent, so pick one you like and stay right on track.

# Pets

Where would people be without their pets?
Probably be out there losing their money somewhere, I bet.

Pets are like people's best friend,
They always show loyalty to you to the very end.

They sometimes can be your only friend and companion;
They stay loyal, and I know that's why they are never considered abandonment.

They often bring on some fun and excitement,
They even can be the bright spot of your day to bring in some enlightenment.

Pets always come and find you when you're in the same room,
I don't care if it's an exotic animal or weird like a baboon.

Pets are friendly animals, just want be around,
They just like attention, or just want to be down,
Even when they do something wrong,
Like pee in your home or bite someone's favorite thong,
But I will say pets are human's best friend.

They will stay by you to the very end.

**Corey Dixon**

# Chapter 5

Corey Dixon

# When Enough is Enough

Some people have different levels of tolerance,

For some it comes down to a lack of patience.

You just get pushed to your limits that make you crawl,

Or people get on your nerves to make you drive up a wall.

When you have had enough, you start to look at your options,

Like a friend, a job, or a girlfriend or boyfriend, and figure is this the end?

You get fed up with saying enough is enough; you're ready to move some on,

Sometimes I wish they made a spray called whoosh be gone!

But when you can't take it no more, then simply don't;

I don't care what you have to do, even grunt.

Then the next person you interact with will catch it all,

Then you'll be there like why are they mad, or who dropped the ball?

Trust me, when you had enough it's a field of no regrets,

And that's the truth, I would bet.

It's like that's all, and you can't even go;

You're just ready to terminate it, to move on to the next show.

So when enough is enough you find a way out,

But never leave room or any error or some doubt.

Corey Dixon

# Moving On

I really don't know what's wrong,

But you get a plateau to where you have to move on.

If some artist read my book, that's a title to a song;

Just remember where you got it from, catchy like thong, thong.

But everyone reaches a point where you have had enough,

So all you can do now is strut your stuff.

Moving on basically means you have had enough,

So just take it how it is, don't try to be Mr. or Ms. Tough.

I know we don't have the patience that Jesus did

'Cause when something happens to us, we, as a whole, be acting like little kids.

Moving on means you had enough tolerance as you can handle, so it's time to go;

So pick up your belongings, leave what didn't work for you, and move to the next show.

### Various Shades of Poetry

'Cause move on means you're tired with what you're encountering;

Even though it may hurt you, you're the person you have to hurt, like a bee sting.

    And this could come from anything, like your job, doing the same thing, or spouse or a wife, over and over,

Like a two-ton vehicle ran you over, like a Land Rover.

But this is nothing but a quick run-through of what has happened, meaning the reason;

Don't fret 'cause everything has its limit when it comes to your season.

**Corey Dixon**

## Spirit States

Some states still have that old spirit in them. Case and point, let's take the state of Missouri. As you see, in today's time, we have the Mike Brown fiasco that includes the police officer named Darren Wilson. Now, when the event occurred a few months back—I believe it was in August 9, 2014—the city of Ferguson erupted in violence, into looting several businesses around the Ferguson area. A big name department store was vandalized, along of several individual shops. But the state has two sides of people protesting—the African American race for Mike Brown, and in other counties, like Arnold, protestors for Officer Wilson. Everyone around the globe knows the slogan "Hands up, don't shoot!" But the officer shot anyways. And it doesn't look like the officer will be facing any charges as of this date.

**Various Shades of Poetry**

# Poem Slave States

It is true some states have made radical changes around the United States, like the majority of the South,

But some states haven't, like Missouri, and still live in the 50's era where the same slave spirit lives with clout.

Even when they started coverage of the Mike Brown story, they showed the person doing wrong, as that would portray a suitable reason for getting shot,

Other African Americans couldn't believe that, and their stomach was sick feeling, having their stomach tied in knots.

For several weeks people was still feeling unease.

But police officers still treated African Americans like we are all were suspects, as if they had some kind of disease.

To even use the little video clip of someone doing wrong, they thought of that as being racially defiant,

So you know how the African American race took that insult and started to riot.

I had a couple of friends that came to show the cause, even I was there in attendance

To show support for this heinous act of Michael Brown and these incidents where news traveled around the globe, and it was definitely tremendous.

But if you do your history, Missouri was a slave state in the past

To where racial profiling still exists, and it will last.

But I not trying to preach to all like I was a pastor and this is the Sunday sermon,

Different states have a bigger possession of demonic demons that patrol city areas.

# Corey Dixon

# **Continued**

Now, they were talking about on the news during this time that Officer Wilson was in total distress over the incident. Meanwhile, they set up a trust fund in his defense since the last time they said anything about the incident. The officer accumulated somewhere about three hundred thousand dollars for lawyers' fees for a court case. Also, so that no one would retaliate against him, he was immediately placed on some type of witness protection plan to protect the shooter who slain another. Only in a slave state you will see this as well. But I only have one question: even if the suspect grabs for your gun once, you have an enemy subdued or the person is throwing up a surrender motion, how is it that you decided to slay the other individual when their hands are in the air? Another question is how come your gun is still out when the person is on their knees saying "Don't shoot." I'm not the smartest person around, but by giving the context clues—hands up, surrendering—I don't see where there needs to be a point of killing anyone. Then, to add insult to injury, the news reported the body laid in the street for hours. The policeman left the scene of the place where this incident took place. If I was an officer, I would have told the chief of what happened anything, but for the Ferguson police department to worry about their officer more than removing the dead body out of the street is just a little bit drastic. And then to get the violence to end, they have to use an African American male to calm the violence down.

# Step Up Your Game

Now, I don't know if someone told you, but you need to step up your game;

Quit acting like you're in high school 'cause it's sure a crying shame.

See, I will make sure I have the last laugh

'Cause you might as well call me a wide receiver like Eric Metcalf;

I see you don't learn new things since I dumped you,

So you can get a better look at this or a better view;

When someone breaks up with you that means something is broken,

That means fix it or you're going to need another token;

That's okay if it takes you time to learn,

As long as you make an attempt from your mistakes you learn;

But now you're too much using the mouth piece you burned,

So tell me, do you know why I left you? So you won't make another U-turn;

I doubt it if you can think and make it that far,

But that's okay; I'll even come and get you if you need a ride in a car,

**Corey Dixon**

> But messing with you was surely a mistake,
>
> And I'll put it all on that if I was a gambling man I can take;
>
> Well, get props for our beautiful baby boy
>
> 'Cause that may be the last time in life if you ever have some joy, T.J.;

So, P.S., you really don't know who you're messing with, but don't worry, you can find out with the money I'll make.

So you go study nursing 'cause you'll need the cake.

## Child Support

Hey, I don't care about no stinking child support,

So guess what? I guess I will see you in court.

Now, I have one question:

When will you start thinking, to learn your lesson?

Well, I'll help you: How do you think you're going to get some money,

When, since the baby was born, I had an accident? Don't you believe that's funny?

Another thing is you so stupid I learned beforehand,

Now I know you wasn't thinking or knew that was the plan.

Now I know how to take you down,

And please believe I am going to brag all through the towns.

This is one of those things I can say, Lucifer, you wasn't thinking,

**Corey Dixon**

You must have been out partying too much or did too much drinking.

See, don't you think it's too ironic I found out before it happened?

Well, just thank the two star players that I call the captains;

Think, just think, you could have made it big and rich like me,

But you don't have an excuse, so you be living with mom and grandmom's,

Or a personal Indian hut, call it a teepee;

So I'm ready for you, bring it on,

And get knocked out just like a bell goes dong!

You don't know but you're making me richer,

But you're too dumb to notice so ask someone else. Did you get the picture?

# Plan

P – Is to have a positive purpose in your plan;

L – To become a lieutenant or higher so you can be the man or woman;

A – Is to achieve more than expected, to become all things;

N – To handle it like it's possible and treat it like it's nothing.

Corey Dixon

# Think

Someone smart told me you always have to think in this world in order to make it,

If you don't it's possible to reach the bottom of the pavement.

You can't make it far if you don't use your noggin

Or still be at home taking laps at your mom or grandma's house, doing some jogging.

Always and always think ahead,

And always even pray to God before you go to bed.

This world ain't here, made for the lucent weak,

Even low class people have to do something, I don't care if they're about to slip off a creek.

To me life's like chess: you have to advance,

And that's a strategy, too; and all is extra, plus the romance.

But in a thinking man's game, it takes strategic plotting;

If you don't think so, you might become of the few that's like a strategic rotten'.

**Various Shades of Poetry**

So, if you ever want to become something, you better start do something, like think,

So you can advance so far ahead you'll know nothing but nice and wool minks.

Corey Dixon

# Stupid

Excuse me, ma'am or woman, do you have to be so stupid?

Can't you be more loving like on Valentine's Day and find cupid?

You see, when you don't have it all, something's just not right,

You say things stupidly if that might make folks fight.

When you're stupid, your brain might be slow

And other people may know it, too, and they might not want to go.

When someone's so stupid they don't stand a chance,

Might not even stand a chance at romance.

Stupid folks are sometimes on a red light,

But their light never changes mentally; that's when something is not right.

All the other person knows is that it's your time to go,

So pack your bags and say to someone else, say Hello;

But it's got to suck when you are stupid

Or be just crazy when someone has to leave you like this;

**Various Shades of Poetry**

It kind of leaves you open, like a sour taste of Sierra Mist.

That means you have to take flight
And leave quickly with all of your might.

But this is for all the folks that are definitely slow:
Just be cool and alright, but everyone don't want to go.

Corey Dixon

# Bad Chick

I'm on the search for a bad chick,

Like someone that I can spend my life with.

I would prefer them tall because I myself am six-nine,

And for me to have someone tall too would be fine (but all heights are welcome).

A bad chick has to have smarts and know what to do with her life

And don't think they need some other guy and to make it be alright.

Now, this chick can't be dumb and has to have smarts,

Like know and pass calculus two and to have some of the nicer arts.

'Cause it's not easy to find a bad chick available

'Cause the good around in my area are taken, like they stay in a stable.

### Various Shades of Poetry

But a chick's got to have goals

And not just be some low life that dances around a pole.


She has to look good, and God broke the mold when they made you;

You look so good they should try to duplicate you and make a carbon copy of you into a crew.


'Cause you know fine and fine meets more,

Like it's a lot of you out there and has more in the store.


And she has to have a brain

So you know she ain't the one to drive you insane.


She'll have to be like the one that's made with a different cloth

And be like one of the ones that aren't messing with stars like Rick Ross.


So, bad chick, where art thou?

Please come down from your cloud,

And your boy then will be so, so proud.

Corey Dixon

# Church

Do you ever think about ever going to church?

And that's right, I said it right, nor did I burp;

Don't you want to know about the person who made you,

At least know your master, the one you have, the choice to choose?

Do you know what He did so you can have a chance?

I can say this: Jesus gave up his life so we can eternally advance.

You see, church is somewhere you go for fellowship,

You even can bring your lady or fellow right on to with you with.

And see, going to church weekly is like a weekly antidote,

You even see people there, too, and they might even write a few notes.

So if you ain't never been, go to service and try it out,

Learn about the Lord & you won't have any doubts.

I think you can actually give yourself back to Christ,

That has to taste better than some food, like your favorite tripe.

So if you never went and you go,

**Various Shades of Poetry**

You're in my area, come to 8901 Pleasant View Drive in Fairview Heights, Illinois—think it's 62207; you're always welcome through Bishop Rex M. Waddell;

Now, if you're in the Columbus, Ohio, area, you should check out Flintridge Missionary Baptist on 3330 Scottwood Road, Columbus, Ohio 43227;

Now if you're in the Chicago area, preferably the suburbs, you have a location to go to, hear the infamous man of God named Smokie Norful; I think you may have heard the name before— location and name of the church is Victory Cathedral Worship Center in Bolingbrook, Illinois, 369 N Weber Road, 60440;

Missourians should check out my new church home, which is Church on the Rock, or cotr.org, and check out the podcast to listen to pastors Mr. and Mrs. Blount; get an awesome word, as well; I believe the address is 900 Birdie Boulevard, 63376.


So if you are in the area, check them out; I'm sure you will not be disappointed!

**Corey Dixon**

# Feeling a Bit Shallow

I'm going to tell you the reason for feeling a bit shallow:

Because one of my ex- girlfriends has moved on and found a man, leaving me a bit hollow.

When I read that, I was in disbelief;

Think, Well, it's been almost seven years, is someone supposed to be discrete?

Just 'cause I left her then without a real-enough reason

Then wanted to come back, I should be hit with the crime of treason.

What was I supposed to think, was she supposed to wait for seven years,

Then I'll get my act together and it ends with an all good that will equal to a bunch of cheers?

Now in this current time and day, I wish it went that away,

But guess what—I'm not going get that bunny right today.

**Various Shades of Poetry**

And if she knew I was ready to even propose,

Because I could have settled down with the one I previously chose,

Now, I end this saying if you have a good one, hold on, too,

Or you can feel like me, get nausea till your face turns blue.

**Corey Dixon**

# Being rejected

Nothing feels like being rejected,

It hurts almost like a cut where you need some antiseptic.

All you want is for the bleeding to stop,

Or to just end it all, or like an explosion goes pop.

That basically means there's no space for you here,

So move on out the way till you get someone to hear.

Other people have been rejected for reasons,

You know everything has its time and place, just like a season.

That basically means we don't need you no more,

Go off and find something else just like a chore.

So you just wait on your day

When you will be accepted, and things will seem okay.

Being rejected is like a release of frustration,

**Various Shades of Poetry**

But millions of people felt it from a relationship, job, and not being accepted across the nation;

But, in the meantime, just work on yourself till you be perfected,

And nobody will throw you away 'cause you're like medicine and will get accepted.

**Corey Dixon**

# **Write**

W – Willing to do whatever you have to do to be where you trying to be;

R – Is remember and rectifying all problems and tasks;

I – Is to be intelligent when coming up with solutions;

T – Is using your thing for teaching and learning a technique;

E – Is to educate others that you may have skill.

Now, you're doing this because you may have skills,

But others will see that, too, as soon as you get a book deal.

# Destiny

Do you really know what is in your destiny?

Is it big, or small—something like a bumblebee?

Does your destiny have purpose?

Is it good or bad, and are you getting nervous?

Destiny is what God intended you to be;

Do you know you are supposed to make it real big on TV?

Now, some know, like some professional athletes;

Other people know they are, too, like professional volleyball players that play on the beach.

See, for Michael Jordan he knew his destiny 'cause he made millions off hooping and shoes;

Along the way of growing up, he probably was getting clues.

So basically, like the Army commercial, Be all that you can be

So you can reach your destiny.

Corey Dixon

# Guide to a Healthy Diet

The first step is to have a daily goal of calories you want to reach—for example, a range from 1200 to 1500.

The second step is to read all nutrition facts to know how many calories you're taking in on whatever it is you're eating, as well as to calculate them at the end of the day to keep track of it.

The third step is to make a workout schedule. Beginners can start out a minimum of once per day. Intermediate people would have a minimum of two times per day. Advanced people would be working out at least three times a day.

Workout times for beginners would be twenty consistent minutes with a two-minute break if needed. Intermediate level would be thirty-five to forty minutes with a five-minute break if needed. Advanced level would be fifty minute to one hour with a seven-minute break if needed. The intermediate and advanced levels can break that time up. For example, the intermediate person can do two twenty-minute workouts one day and still equal forty minutes, just like the advanced person can break the workout into three twenty-minute sessions.

The most challenging stage is for the beginner level. This is based on what type of physical shape you are in when you start working out. Depending on how much strength you have, you can push yourself to work out for twenty minutes with no breaks! It's even more of a challenges if you haven't worked out in a while because your muscles have to be worked back into a rhythm, so some soreness may occur. But the good thing is that the soreness is only temporary. Once you get to the next level, you will be working out full speed.

The next thing would be to set up boundaries for yourself—for example, if you eat some chips. According to the nutrition facts, the average is 140 calories for about 11 to 14 chips. At the most, you should eat between 22 and 28 chips. Calorie-wise that's only coming out to be 280 calories based off the example, which leaves 900 to 1300 calories to play with for the rest of the day. This leaves enough for two to three meals and another snack, and that's for beginners.

Now, for the immediate and advanced people, it can be like 200 fewer calories. A good 250 to 400 is borderline per sitting. Anything past 450 calories in a sitting is almost a third of your daily intake goal. You still can eat it, just add a short workout to your day. A gym membership would be the best route to go. If you don't have one, then workout tapes for thirty minutes would be a very good option for you.

The average intake to maintain the same weight is either 2000 or 2500 calories. So you're instantly cutting out between 500-1000

**Corey Dixon**

calories without even working out! That will get the job done right there. When you add your workout routine to that, you will see results greater, better, quicker.

Even if you don't go over the calories in your goal, that is okay. Just make sure you work that off the extra calories to maintain your goal number.

Another helpful tip would be this: say your favorite snack is chips. What you can do is buy the smallest version of them, like a thirty-cent bag. The bag is small, so you know you're taking a smaller amount of calories. This is applicable to any snackfood you like to eat primarily. Many other plans tell you to cut this off or cut that out, but that's not a 100 percent necessity. Although cutting away is the best effect, all you need is some self-discipline, like the boundaries that I explained earlier, and you will be on your way.

"The key to a successful diet is balance."

                                          Corey Dixon

# Various Shades of Poetry

First and foremost, I have to acknowledge and thank my Father in Heaven for making all this possible and to spare me with my life. I might as well thank Him for my future endeavors, too, because as long as He is in it I will be alright.

Second, I have to go through my family, like all of the Dixons, even though most of you didn't know I was writing a book. But to complete any kind of book is a big task, regardless of who it is. To my two cousins, hey, I might just earn airfare out there to come see you all soon.

The next three I have to get a major shout-out to is my old G, Grandmother, for watching me ever since I was small. My (niezel) sister and my mom, and can't forget my bro-in-law, too. Now where would I be?

Of course, I have to give all the Fords love, too: my grandma on that side, and aunts and uncles, down to my cuzzos.

I will like to end this out in fashion, with, of course, a prayer. Then the book will come to an end. I have to add the last two as the most important people my life: little man, J-fizzle, Jaylin, and my partner in crime, the future Mrs. Dixon whose initials are T.A.J!

Corey Dixon

Copyright © 2015 by Corey Dixon
All rights reserved.

Green Ivy Publishing
1 Lincoln Centre
18W140 Butterfield Road
Suite 1500
Oakbrook Terrace IL 60181-4843

ISBN: 978-1-942901-33-4

www.ingramcontent.com/pod-product-compliance
Lightning Source LLC
Chambersburg PA
CBHW071616080526
44588CB00010B/1152